"Bring the Classics to Life"

BLACK BEAUTY

LEVEL 2

Series Designer
Philip J. Solimene

Editor
Deborah Tiersch-Allen

EDCON

Story Adapter
Jacqueline Nightingale

Author
Anna Sewell

Copyright © 1997
A/V Concepts Corp.
30 Montauk Blvd, Oakdale NY 11769
info@edconpublishing.com
1-888-553-3266
Visit our Web site at: www.edconpublishing.com

Printed in U.S.A.
ISBN# 0-931334-51-9

CONTENTS

Words Used   4,5

WORDS USED

Story 1	Story 2	Story 3	Story 4	Story 5
KEY WORDS				
brother	cage	family	drink	band
carry	done	reach	face	crawl
drop	drive	stand	foot	listen
land	follow	threw	kind	visit
sent	fox	wait	king	whale
wear	knock	write	love	world
NECESSARY WORDS				
dead	bite	bridge	blanket	bar
manners	free	job	doctor	whip
master	short	smoke	felt	
saddle	carriage		rub	
star			sick	

WORDS USED

Story 6	Story 7	Story 8	Story 9	Story 10
KEY WORDS				
branch	arm	finish	dirty	hope
need	bad	kitchen	feather	jolly
smell	because	later	felt	lion
strong	early	left	great	sky
supper	food	poor	maybe	song
wonderful	shout	sign	sheep	stairs
NECESSARY WORDS				
	understand	cab	crash	load
		war	hospital	strength
			station	
			vote	

MY FIRST HOME

PREPARATION

Key Words

brother   (bruᴛʜ ′ ər)   a boy who has the same father and mother as another boy or girl
My sister and <u>brother</u> walk me to school every day.

carry   (ker ′ ē)   to take from one place to another
I will <u>carry</u> that bag to the car for you.

drop   (drop)   to let something fall
Do not <u>drop</u> the puzzle I just put together.

land   (land)   a country or place where people live; the parts of the earth not covered by water
That part of the <u>land</u> has many trees.

sent   (sent)   to have had someone or something go somewhere
My mother <u>sent</u> me to the store to buy eggs.

wear   (wer, war)   to have on; to put on
My father will <u>wear</u> his new shirt to work.

MY FIRST HOME

Necessary Words

dead   (ded)

no longer living
> *When the cold winter came, the flowers were all <u>dead</u>.*

manners   (man ′ ərs)

way of acting
> *The children showed their good <u>manners</u> by sitting quietly during the show.*

master   (mas ′ tər)

a person who is the head of something
> *The <u>master</u> of the school liked to talk to all the children.*

saddle   (sad ′ l)

seat for a rider on a horse's back
> *The man put a fine <u>saddle</u> on his horse and got ready for a long ride.*

star   (stär)

a shape with five or six points
> *The teacher put a <u>star</u> on my paper to show that I had done good work.*

Animals

Darkie   is a young horse who is growing up on a farm with his mother. He is the horse that this story is mostly about.

Pet   is Darkie's mother and a fine horse.

People

Squire Gordon   is the master of a nearby farm who wants to own Darkie.

MY FIRST HOME

My mother and I would run around the farm all day.

Preview:
1. Read the name of the story.
2. Look at the picture.
3. Read the sentence under the picture.
4. Read the first two paragraphs of the story.
5. Then answer the following question.

You learned from your preview that the story is being told by

_____ a. a horse.

_____ b. a man.

_____ c. a child.

_____ d. a mother.

Turn to the Comprehension Check on page 10 for the right answer.

Now read the story.

Read to find out how the young horse's life will change.

MY FIRST HOME

My first home was a farm on a land of green grass and high trees. My master lived in a big house near the road.

At first I lived on my mother's milk. We ran around the field all day. When I got a little older, I could eat grass. Then my mother went out to work. Because I had no brother, I would run with the other horses. What fun we had!

My mother told me of my father's good name. Most of the people in this part of the land had heard of him. She said I must carry my head high and keep my good manners.

My master was a good man and a friend to all his horses. He called my mother Pet. I was called Darkie. He liked us best of all his horses.

Just before I was two years old, I saw something that was most surprising. It was in the spring. We heard the cry of many dogs.

"They have found a rabbit," my mother said. "Soon we will see them running by."

A rabbit went past us. Many dogs and men on horses were on her tail. The rabbit could not get out of the garden. The dogs were all over her. I saw her head drop. A man picked up the prize—a dead rabbit.

Suddenly, some men went running over to a boy in the grass. It was Squire Gordon's boy. He was dead when his head met the hard ground.

Soon after, I saw that a horse had dropped to the ground. It had a broken leg. We heard a big bang and the horse was gone too. So much had been lost over one little rabbit and the games men played.

My mother was very sad. I was to find out later that the fallen horse had been my brother.

As time went by, my coat began to get blacker. One of my feet was white and I had a pretty star on my head.

Squire Gordon came to look me over when I was four years old. He wanted me for his farm. My master said he would train me for Squire Gordon.

Training is when a horse must get used to carrying a man on his back and wearing a saddle. I also had to wear horse shoes on my feet. In time, I would get used to all the things a horse must do.

My master was my friend and he took his time with me. At last the day came when he got on my back. At first I did not like it. But I wanted to please him so I went well.

Another part of my training was to get used to loud trains. I was sent to a farm where the train ran close to the field. I did not like the loud noise, but I soon got used to it and did not mind.

The time came to say good-by to my mother and my master. My mother told me to do my best and please my new master. She told me to carry my head high and keep up our good name.

MY FIRST HOME

COMPREHENSION CHECK

Choose the best answer.

1. The name of the young horse is
    _____ a.   Pet.
    _____ b.   Squire Gordon.
    _____ c.   Darkie.
    _____ d.   Rabbit.

2. Darkie's mother
    _____ a.   was Squire Gordon's newest horse.
    _____ b.   did not like running with the other horses.
    _____ c.   liked to hunt rabbits.
    _____ d.   cared for Darkie very much.

3. Darkie and Pet's master
    _____ a.   was a good and kind man.
    _____ b.   treated them very badly.
    _____ c.   wanted to get rid of them.
    _____ d.   did not have much money.

4. Rabbit hunting
    _____ a.   was fun for horses and rabbits.
    _____ b.   was a safe thing to do.
    _____ c.   was dangerous for men and horses.
    _____ d.   was stopped after the horse fell.

5. Darkie
    _____ a.   was all black.
    _____ b.   had a star on his head.
    _____ c.   broke his leg in a race.
    _____ d.   was not happy on the farm.

6. Darkie was sent to a farm where a train ran by
    _____ a.   so he would learn to run faster.
    _____ b.   because it was easier to get places.
    _____ c.   so he would get used to the loud noise.
    _____ d.   because he was being sent away.

7. Wearing a saddle
    _____ a.   was fun for Darkie.
    _____ b.   made Darkie hold his head high.
    _____ c.   made Darkie very sad.
    _____ d.   was something Darkie had to get used to.

8. Darkie was told by his mother
    _____ a.   to carry his head high and keep his good name.
    _____ b.   to stay far away from Squire Gordon.
    _____ c.   not to carry men on his back.
    _____ d.   to wear his shoes and saddle at all times.

9. Another name for this story could be
    _____ a.   "A New Beginning."
    _____ b.   "Home Sweet Home."
    _____ c.   "Training Horses."
    _____ d.   "Chasing Rabbits."

10. This story is mainly about
    _____ a.   two horses and a rabbit.
    _____ b.   a young horse growing up.
    _____ c.   how to run after rabbits.
    _____ d.   living on a farm.

Check your answers with the key on page 67.

MY FIRST HOME

VOCABULARY CHECK

brother	carry	drop	land	sent	wear

I. Sentences to Finish

Fill in the blank in each sentence with the correct key word from the box above.

1. Please_____this plate over to the table.

2. My_____and I love to play baseball in the park.

3. Maria comes from a far away_____.

4. If you_____that box of dishes, they will break.

5. Can I_____my new dress to the party?

6. Peter_____away for a free toy.

II. Mixed-up Words

First, unscramble the letters in Column A to spell out the key words. Then, match the key words with the right meaning in column B by drawing a line.

Column A	Column B
1. racyr _____	a. a boy who has the same mother or father as another boy or girl
2. tsen _____	b. to take from one place to another
3. raew _____	c. to put on
4. rpod _____	d. a country or place
5. adnl _____	e. to let something fall
6. trehrob _____	f. to have someone or something go somewhere

Check your answers with the key on page 69.

This page may be reproduced for classroom use.

BIRTWICK PARK

PREPARATION

Key Words

cage   (kāj)   a place with bars to keep animals in
The monkey sat in his cage at the zoo.

done   (dun)   to finish something
When you are done with your work, you may go outside.

drive   (drīv)   to make a car, bus or truck go along
My mother wanted to drive us to school on the rainy day.

follow   (fol ' ō)   to go after someone or something
All the children in the class had to follow the leader around the room.

fox   (foks)   a wild animal like a dog, but with a long, bushy tail
The men rode horses into the woods after a fox.

knock   (nok)   to bang on something and make noise
My friends knock on my window in the morning to get me out of bed.
to hit or bump into something
The boy tried not to knock over his mother's good vase.

BIRTWICK PARK

Necessary Words

bite   (bīt)   to cut into something with one's teeth
> *I took a big bite out of an apple.*

free   (frē)   to do, act or think as one pleases
> *I was as free as a bird when I was out in the woods.*

short   (shôrt)   not long; not tall
> *The horse had a short tail and could not brush the flies off his back.*

carriage   (kar ′ ij)   a kind of wagon used to carry people. Some are pulled by horses.
> *We rode through the park in a carriage pulled by two beautiful black horses.*

People

Mrs. Gordon   is Squire Gordon's wife.

John   is the barn master and the man that cares for Black Beauty on Squire Gordon's farm.

Animals

Ginger   is the horse that pulls the carriage with Black Beauty on Squire Gordon's farm.

Merrylegs   is a sweet pony that lives on the farm that is Black Beauty's new home.

Things

loose box   a large box-like room in a barn, where a horse can move around freely.

BIRTWICK PARK

It was here, on Squire Gordon's farm, that I would get my new name.

Preview:
1. Read the name of the story
2. Look at the picture.
3. Read the sentence under the picture.
4. Read the first three paragraphs of the story.
5. Then answer the following question.

You learned from your preview that
_____ a. the young horse's new home seemed to be a nice place.
_____ b. the young horse had to live in a small place.
_____ c. the young horse ran away when it was time to leave.
_____ d. the young horse did not like people very much.

Turn to the Comprehension Check on page 16 for the right answer.

Now read the story.

Read to find out about the young horse's new friends.

BIRTWICK PARK

In May, a man from Squire Gordon's farm came to take me away. My master said good-bye and I put my nose in his hand.

Squire Gordon's farm was like a pretty picture. There were large trees, a big house and pretty gardens.

I went to live in a large barn with many other horses. I was put into a loose box. This was a fine surprise to me. A loose box is the best home for a horse in a barn. You have far more room to move around. Some of the other horses were in little rooms like cages.

I made some new friends. One was a pony named Merrylegs, and another, a horse named Ginger. Ginger let me know that it was I who put her out of the loose box and into her cage. Merrylegs told me Ginger liked to bite people so she was put out of the box.

John was the barn master in my new home. A better man could not be found. He took good care of me and brushed me until I was soft and smooth. He was a good friend.

When I was fitted with my saddle, my new master was ready to ride me. After our ride, he told Mrs. Gordon that I would do just fine. I hoped we would not ever follow along with the other horses to look for a fox or a rabbit.

It was at this place that I was to get my name—Black Beauty.

Ginger and I had to pull the carriage. We did this next to one another. It was hard not to knock into each other, but we did our best. We got along fine. I found that she did all her work. I never wished for a better horse next to me. When we were done with our drive, the master would give us each an apple.

Merrylegs and I were fast to make friends with one another. He was a very happy pony with a little nose and short legs like a fox.

One day, when Ginger and I were alone under a tree, we had a long talk. She said no one had ever been good to her. All her masters were not like the one I had. That was why she liked to bite people.

The only thing I missed here was being free. But all the people were good and I would try to make the best of it.

On Sundays we could run around and have fun after our drive. When we were done running, we would knock apples off the trees and eat them.

I had the best rider on the farm on my back—Mrs. Gordon. She had a very light hand. I was happy to take her for a ride. We would follow the master.

This farm was a good one for any horse to live and work on.

BIRTWICK PARK

COMPREHENSION CHECK

Choose the best answer.

1. Darkie went to Squire Gordon's farm in the
   ____ a. spring.
   ____ b. summer.
   ____ c. winter.
   ____ d. fall.

2. The barn master was
   ____ a. Ginger.
   ____ b. Merrylegs.
   ____ c. Mrs. Gordon.
   ____ d. John.

3. Darkie's new name was
   ____ a. Ginger Gordon.
   ____ b. John Merrylegs.
   ____ c. Black Beauty.
   ____ d. Blackie Gordon.

4. Ginger liked to bite people because
   ____ a. she was always hungry.
   ____ b. her saddle did not fit well.
   ____ c. she thought it was a fun thing to do.
   ____ d. she had not been treated well in the past.

5. Black Beauty
   ____ a. was easy to get along with.
   ____ b. was a mean, fresh horse.
   ____ c. always wanted things done his way.
   ____ d. was not really very happy anywhere.

6. When Ginger and Black Beauty pulled the wagon,
   ____ a. Merrylegs tried to come between them.
   ____ b. they worked well together.
   ____ c. Ginger did not do her part.
   ____ d. Black Beauty was always tired and hot.

7. Most of all, Black Beauty missed
   ____ a. chasing rabbits.
   ____ b. his favorite apple tree.
   ____ c. his friends at the old farm.
   ____ d. being free.

8. Mrs. Gordon
   ____ a. liked to ride Black Beauty.
   ____ b. enjoyed riding Ginger.
   ____ c. did not ride very well.
   ____ d. wanted to get a new horse.

9. Another name for this story could be
   ____ a. "A New Home and a New Name."
   ____ b. "Ginger and Merrylegs."
   ____ c. "Working Very Hard."
   ____ d. "Thinking of Home."

10. This story is mainly about
    ____ a. learning to work on a farm.
    ____ b. making new friends.
    ____ c. getting used to a new home.
    ____ d. living on a farm.

Check your answers with the key on page 67.

BIRTWICK PARK

VOCABULARY CHECK

cage	done	drive	follow	fox	knock

I. Sentences to Finish

Fill in the blank in each sentence with the correct key word from the box above.

1. I like to watch the lions in their _____ at the zoo.

2. Bobby's puppy always tries to _____ _____ him to school.

3. The _____ is a funny animal.

4. Listen! I hear a _____ at the door.

5. Can your mother _____ us to the circus?

6. We can go to the park when I'm _____ eating lunch.

II. Word Search

Circle the hidden words in the letters below. They may be written from left to right or up and down. One word, that is not a key word, has been done for you.

```
M  H  Z  L  N  H  O  M  P
Y  E  M  B  E  R  F  B  S
D  U  F  O  L  L  O  W  T
R  F  E  M  R  Y  X  D  D
I  Y  E  H  V  M  B  E  O
V  Q  K  N  O  C  K  B  N
E  L  L  I  P  A  N  C  E
F  I  V  R  D  C  A  G  E
A  P  P  L  E  M  U  N  D
```

Check your answers with the key on page 69.

THE FIRE

PREPARATION

Key Words

family   (fam ′ ə lē)   a mother, father and their children
Paul and his family went on the picnic with us.

reach   (rēch)   to touch; to stretch out
It was difficult to reach the book because it was in a high place.
get to; come to
We will reach the lake when we come to the end of this trail.

stand   (stand)   to be on your feet
I had to stand on the line in the store for a long time.
to go through something that is hard to take
I could not stand the loud noises from the cars and trucks, so I closed the window.

threw   (thrü)   to send up into the air (past tense of throw)
The boy threw his hat up after winning the game.

wait   (wāt)   to stay in one spot until someone comes or something happens
We always wait for the bus on the corner.

write   (rīt)   to form words by putting letters down on paper or on a board
I told my friend that I would write her a letter very soon.

THE FIRE

Necessary Words

bridge   (brij)   something built over a river or road so that people, cars or trains can get across
We had to drive over a <u>bridge</u> that went across the water to get to the next town.

job   (job)   work that is done for pay
My new <u>job</u> is putting boxes on trucks.

smoke   (smōk)   what goes into the air from something which is burning or has burned
It was hard to get any air because the room was full of <u>smoke</u>.

People

James   is a boy who helps in the barn where Black Beauty lives.

Joe Green   is a boy who comes to take James' place in the barn on Squire Gordon's farm.

Things

dogcart   is a small, open carriage with two seats that are back to back. The dogcart is pulled by a horse.

THE FIRE

When I came out of my sleep, my nose told me there was smoke in the barn.

Preview: 1. Read the name of the story.
2. Look at the picture.
3. Read the sentence under the picture.
4. Read the first two paragraphs of the story.
5. Then answer the following question.

You learned from your preview that
____ a. Black Beauty was enjoying his night ride.
____ b. bridges are never safe to cross.
____ c. Black Beauty was out in a bad storm.
____ d. Master and Mrs. Gordon were mean people.

Turn to the Comprehension Check on page 22 for the right answer.

Now read the story.

Read to find out if Black Beauty and Ginger are safe after some dangerous happenings.

THE FIRE

The more I lived on Squire Gordon's farm, the more I liked it. There were no finer people anywhere than Master and Mrs. Gordon. If I were not a horse, I would write a book about all the good they did for animals and people in this land.

One day my master had a long buying trip to take. I would pull the dogcart. It was raining very hard. We were just about to reach the bridge, when a man came running. He threw up his hands to stop us. He said the water under the bridge was very high. It would be a very bad night.

We went on to the town. I had a long wait for my master and I had to stand in one place. I heard my master tell another man that he had never driven in such rain as this before.

On the way home the rain was just as bad. A tree went down before us on the road. We would have to take the bridge home.

Just as I put my feet on the bridge, I stopped. I could tell something was not right. John got down and came to my head. Soon a man came out. "Wait," he said, "the bridge is no good!"

We were just about to reach the master's door, when Mrs. Gordon came running out. She threw her hands up to us. My master was very happy with me for keeping us off the bridge, and he told her so. John gave me much to eat that night, and I was ready for a good sleep.

My master got a letter asking for a good barn hand to train. He talked to John about asking James to go. John said James was a good boy and he would train him for the job. John would miss James very much, but he would not stand in his way.

One day, James had to drive Master and Mrs. Gordon to visit a family that lived far away. He was told to bring Ginger and me to a barn. We would eat and sleep there for the night.

I did not know how long I had been sleeping. When I came out of my sleep, my nose told me there was a fire in the barn. There was smoke all over and I did not know how long I could stand it in there.

James came and walked me out. Then he ran back for Ginger. Squire Gordon was happy with James. He said he would write a letter saying James was ready for his new job.

A boy named Joe Green came to stand in for James. He had much training to do, but this was the best farm for any man, boy, or animal to live on.

THE FIRE

COMPREHENSION CHECK

Choose the best answer.

Preview Answer:

c. Black Beauty was out in a bad storm.

1. On Squire Gordon's farm, Black Beauty
   ____ a. liked only John because he fed him.
   ____ b. thought Squire Gordon did not like him.
   ____ c. felt that he was being treated very well.
   ____ d. planned to run away when the rain stopped.

2. Black Beauty stopped before crossing the bridge because
   ____ a. he knew that something was not right.
   ____ b. he heard someone call out his name.
   ____ c. he knew an easier way to go home.
   ____ d. he was being very fresh to John.

3. When Black Beauty and Master Gordon got home that rainy night, Mrs. Gordon was
   ____ a. sleeping and did not want to get up.
   ____ b. happy to see that they were all right.
   ____ c. angry that they got her out of bed.
   ____ d. sad that the bridge was washed out.

4. John
   ____ a. was going to leave because he got a better job.
   ____ b. cared very much about Black Beauty and James.
   ____ c. thought Black Beauty was too good for the Gordons.
   ____ d. believed that James was not a good barn hand.

5. Black Beauty
   ____ a. was a smart and careful horse.
   ____ b. was always afraid of something.
   ____ c. was not liked by the other horses.
   ____ d. was not strong enough on long rides.

6. When the fire started, James
   ____ a. ran to get help.
   ____ b. did not know what to do.
   ____ c. only got Ginger out.
   ____ d. acted quickly.

7. After James got the horses out of the barn,
   ____ a. Black Beauty got very sick.
   ____ b. Squire Gordon was happy with him.
   ____ c. Ginger ran back to get her friend.
   ____ d. the barn master gave him a job.

8. Working as a barn hand
   ____ a. was mostly fun and games.
   ____ b. was only a job for men.
   ____ c. did not take very much time.
   ____ d. took a lot of thought and care.

9. Another name for this story could be
   ____ a. "Two Close Calls."
   ____ b. "John and James."
   ____ c. "Visiting Friends."
   ____ d. "Horses Think Fast."

10. This story is mainly about
    ____ a. how a fire almost kills Black Beauty.
    ____ b. a few dangerous happenings.
    ____ c. what happens when James takes over.
    ____ d. getting Joe ready for his new job.

Check your answers with the key on page 67.

THE FIRE

VOCABULARY CHECK

family	reach	stand	threw	wait	write

I. Sentences to Finish

Fill in the blank in each sentence with the correct key word from the box above.

1. My brother _____ the ball to me.

2. We will _____ the park before it gets dark.

3. I had to _____ because all the chairs were taken.

4. My _____ likes to take a trip every summer.

5. Will you _____ for me at the bus stop?

6. Susan did not remember to _____ her name on her paper.

II. Cross Word Puzzle

Use the words from the box above to fill in the puzzle. The meanings below will help you choose the right words.

Across

1. get to; come to

3. to stay in one spot

5. to have sent up in the air

Down

2. a mother, father and their children

3. to form words by putting letters on paper

4. to be on your feet

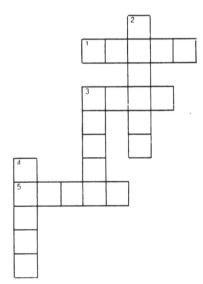

Check your answers with the key on page 69.

THE DOCTOR

PREPARATION

Key Words

drink   (dringk)   to swallow something like water or milk
We took along some cold water to drink on our long walk.

face   (fās)   the front of your head
The girl in the picture has a pretty face and a nice smile.
meet bravely
It was hard to face all the people and say my lines in the play.

foot   (fut)   the part of your body at the end of your leg
The baby put one foot in front of the other and began to walk.

kind   (kīnd)   to do good; be nice
The teacher was kind to all the children in her class.

king   (king)   a man who is the head of a country
The small boy would grow up to be king some day.

love   (luv)   a strong liking for someone or something
I love my family very much.

THE DOCTOR

Necessary Words

blanket (blang ′ kit) a soft, heavy covering used to keep people or animals warm
I pulled the <u>blanket</u> over my body to keep warm on the cold night.

doctor (dok ′ t ər) a person who cares for sick people
The <u>doctor</u> told me that I would be feeling better soon.

felt (felt) to have had a feeling
I <u>felt</u> hurt by what my friend said to me.

rub (rub) move one's hand or an object over the top of someone or something
I had to <u>rub</u> hard to get the dirt off my arms.

sick (sik) not well
Because the girl was <u>sick</u>, she had to stay in bed for a week.

THE DOCTOR

John and I got to the doctor's house in town as fast as we could.

Preview:
1. Read the name of the story.
2. Look at the picture.
3. Read the sentence under the picture.
4. Read the first three paragraphs of the story.
5. Then answer the following question.

You learned from your preview that
____ a. Black Beauty was very sick.
____ b. Black Beauty and John had an important job to do.
____ c. John was taking Black Beauty away from the Gordon s.
____ d. Mrs. Gordon was going on a trip.
Turn to the Comprehension Check on page 28 for the right answer.

Now read the story.

Read to find out what happens to Black Beauty after his long ride.

THE DOCTOR

"Get up, Beauty!" called John, the barn master.

I got up on my legs in a hurry. John put the saddle on my back and got ready to go.

Master Gordon told John to ride fast and bring back the doctor. Mrs. Gordon was very sick.

I did my best to get us there as fast as I could. My love for my master and Mrs. Gordon made my legs go faster.

It was three in the morning when we came to the doctor's door. John told the doctor about Mrs. Gordon. He said he would hurry, but he could not take his horse. It had been out all day.

John told the doctor to ride me back to the farm. The doctor was a kind old man, but not as light as John, and not nearly as good a rider.

When we got to the farm, the doctor went into the house. Joe Green took me to the barn. I could hardly walk and I was very hot. My right foot was hurt. Joe rubbed me down all over, but he did not put on my blanket. He gave me some cold water to drink. Thinking he had done a good job, he went away.

I was getting colder and I hurt even more. I wished for my blanket and John. John had to walk home, so it would be a long time before he could help me.

When John came into the barn, I let out a cry. John did not have to be told how I felt. His love for horses made him know just what to do. He put my blanket over me and made me drink something hot. Then he put his kind hands on my face. These things made me feel a little better.

John was most unhappy with Joe. "That silly boy," John said, over and over again.

I was very sick, so John stayed with me day and night. My master came to see me. Had I not been so fast to bring the doctor that night, Mrs. Gordon would not have made it to the morning.

The horse doctor came to see me. He looked me over from head to foot. I felt like a king with so many people trying to make me better.

One night, Joe Green's father asked John to say something nice to Joe. Joe could not face anyone. Joe's father asked John to understand why the boy did what he did. Joe did not know any better. With training, he would get to know all there was to know about horses.

John was so sad that he did not want to listen at first. Then he said he would talk to Joe.

I did get better in time and I went back to my old ways. From time to time we heard that Mrs. Gordon was sick.

Then we got bad news. The Gordon family would have to move where it was hot, so Mrs. Gordon could get better.

I felt like a king at this farm after three happy years. I would miss this place very much. Ginger and I would have to say good-bye to all our friends, our master, and John.

THE DOCTOR

COMPREHENSION CHECK

Choose the best answer.

1. John and Black Beauty got to the doctor's house
   _____ a.   at three in the morning.
   _____ b.   in the middle of the afternoon.
   _____ c.   early in the evening.
   _____ d.   around midnight.

2. Black Beauty brought the doctor to see
   _____ a.   Squire Gordon.
   _____ b.   Joe.
   _____ c.   John.
   _____ d.   Mrs. Gordon.

3. When Black Beauty got home,
   _____ a.   he felt good about helping the doctor.
   _____ b.   he was hot and hurt.
   _____ c.   he wanted something cold to drink.
   _____ d.   he wanted to see Joe.

4. John
   _____ a.   thought Joe had done a good job.
   _____ b.   told Joe what he did was mean.
   _____ c.   was sad and worried about Black Beauty.
   _____ d.   knew Black Beauty would be all right.

5. Many people came to see Black Beauty because
   _____ a.   he was a big star.
   _____ b.   he was very sick.
   _____ c.   they wanted to take him home.
   _____ d.   they were seeing the Gordons.

6. Because of Black Beauty,
   _____ a.   the Gordons had to move away.
   _____ b.   Mrs. Gordon had a bad fall.
   _____ c.   John was able to keep his job on the farm.
   _____ d.   the doctor was able to help Mrs. Gordon.

7. Joe Green
   _____ a.   felt badly that he had not helped Black Beauty·
   _____ b.   saw that Black Beauty was hurt and tired.
   _____ c.   knew just what to do to help Black Beauty.
   _____ d.   did not care about Black Beauty.

8. The horses had to go to another farm because
   _____ a.   they had not done a good job at the Gordon's place.
   _____ b.   Mrs. Gordon was sick and the family had to move.
   _____ c.   there had been a fire at the Gordons.
   _____ d.   John had found a new job far away.

9. Another name for this story could be
   _____ a.   "King of the Barn."
   _____ b.   "Black Beauty and Joe."
   _____ c.   "Helping Mrs. Gordon."
   _____ d.   "The Gordon Family."

10. This story is mainly about
   _____ a.   Black Beauty's love for the Gordons.
   _____ b.   a doctor who makes house calls.
   _____ c.   what to do if a horse gets sick.
   _____ d.   training a new barn hand.

Check your answers with the key on page 67.

THE DOCTOR

VOCABULARY CHECK

drink	face	foot	kind	king	love

I. Sentences to Finish

Fill in the blank in each sentence with the correct key word from the box above.

1. I like to_____milk with my dinner.

2. The_____was a good man and a friend to all.

3. My_____was red because I had run all the way home.

4. Because my shoe was too small, it made a mark on my_____.

5. I am always_____to animals.

6. I_____to read books that have happy endings.

II. Matching

Write the letter of the correct meaning from Column B next to the key word in Column A.

Column A	Column B
_____ 1. drink	a. the front of your head
_____ 2. foot	b. to be good
_____ 3. love	c. the man who is the head of a country
_____ 4. king	d. to swallow something like water
_____ 5. kind	e. the part of your body at the end of your leg
_____ 6. face	f. a strong liking for someone or something

Check your answers with the key on page 70.

MY NEW HOME

PREPARATION

Key Words

band	(band)	a long, thin piece of paper, cloth or leather used as a trim or something else *My dress has a wide, yellow band around the middle.* a group of people together (playing music or acting) *We like to go see the rock band play their music.*
crawl	(krôl)	to move along slowly on your hands and knees like a baby *I had to crawl on the floor to look for the missing pin.*
listen	(lis ′ n)	to hear things *We like to listen to the children sing.*
visit	(viz ′ it)	to go to see someone, or be with people for a little while *Will you visit me in my new home?*
whale	(hwāl)	a very large animal, shaped like a fish, that lives in the ocean *We saw a whale do tricks at the water show.*
world	(wėrld)	the earth *I write to a girl who lives on the other side of the world.*

MY NEW HOME

Necessary Words

bar	(bär)	a place where people can buy drinks and sometimes food *After the game, the players went to have a drink at the bar.*
whip	(hwip)	thing to hit with, like a stick *The man used a whip to make the horse go faster.*

People

Lady Anne is the girl on the farm who likes to ride Black Beauty.

Reuben Smith is the man left behind to take care of all the horses on the farm when the family goes away for a little while.

Things

check rein is a strap used to keep a horse's head high.

MY NEW HOME

The check reins were pulled up so high that we could not move our heads.

Preview: 1. Read the name of the story.
2. Look at the picture.
3. Read the sentence under the picture.
4. Read the first two paragraphs of the story.
5. Then answer the following question.

You learned from your preview that
____a. the new barn master is a mean man.
____b. John does not care about the horses anymore.
____c. Ginger and Black Beauty are no longer together.
____d. Black Beauty and Ginger are in a new home.

Turn to the Comprehension Check on page 34 for the right answer.

Now read the story.

Read to find out how Black Beauty feels about his new home.

MY NEW HOME

John put saddles on Ginger and me, and took us to our new home. It would be a new world for us. We were taken to the barn and put into boxes next to one another.

John talked to our new barn master. It was hard to listen to what was being said, but we did hear a little. John said I was the best horse any man could want. Ginger would be good if he was kind to her. John told him we never had a checkrein on us. The barn master told John that all the horses on this farm had to wear them.

John said a sad good-bye and we never saw him again.

Our job on the farm was to pull the carriage. The woman of the house said we had to have our heads high at all times. A checkrein was put on us to keep our heads up.

Each day, the bands on the checkrein were pulled higher than the day before. Since we could not use our heads to pull, we had to work our legs and backs too hard. It hurt me and made me sad, but I kept my good manners.

One day the bands were pulled higher than Ginger could stand. She kicked so hard the carriage went over. She would never pull the carriage again.

One spring day the family went away for a visit. Lady Anne liked to ride me all the time. But this day she wanted to try a different horse. A small boy made a big noise with a whip. Lady Anne's horse jumped and took off down the road. Her friend ran out of the house and jumped on my back. We ran down the road after them. We went as fast as we could, but it was hard to catch up.

When we found my lady she was on the ground. I wished she would crawl or walk. She did nothing. The doctor was called. When she was on her feet again, Lady Anne was told not to ride any other horse but me. Once again I was happy in my little world.

The barn master had to go for a visit out of town. A man named Reuben Smith was to take care of the band of horses in the barn. He had a love for horses and was liked by all. There was one sad thing about Reuben—he liked to drink.

One night, Reuben took me for a ride to a bar called the White Lion. Reuben must have drank like a whale in the bar that night. When he came out, he did not see that one of my shoes was coming off.

We were riding home so fast that I lost my shoe. The pain was more than I could stand. My feet gave way, and I was down on the ground. Reuben was on the ground close by.

I had to crawl to the grass. I listened for some noise. It was a long time before anyone came. Then I heard Ginger coming with a rider.

Reuben was dead. I will never get the pain of the long walk home that night out of my head.

MY NEW HOME

COMPREHENSION CHECK

Choose the best answer.

1. Black Beauty's job on the farm was
____ a. to keep his head high.
____ b. to visit Lady Anne.
____ c. to take care of Reuben.
____ d. to pull the carriage.

2. When Black Beauty's checkrein was
pulled up, he
____ a. kicked over the carriage.
____ b. would not hold his head up.
____ c. did not like it, but showed good manners.
____ d. would not come out of the barn to work.

3. The lady at Black Beauty's new home
____ a. thought checkreins were not right.
____ b. did not care about the horses.
____ c. was a very kind person.
____ d. did not like riding in the wagon.

4. The day Lady Anne rode a different horse
____ a. she got rid of Black Beauty.
____ b. she had a nice ride.
____ c. she made a new friend.
____ d. she fell and got hurt.

5. Black Beauty thought Lady Anne was
____ a. kind and loving.
____ b. mean and fresh.
____ c. wild and loud.
____ d. pretty and quiet.

6. Reuben Smith
____ a. talked too much.
____ b. was really a good man.
____ c. owned a bar called the White Lion.
____ d. did not really care about horses.

7. The night Reuben took Black Beauty for a ride, they
____ a. went to a bar called the White Lion.
____ b. went to a house by the sea.
____ c. went to a park near the farm.
____ d. went to a zoo to see white lions.

8. At the end of this story
____ a. Ginger cannot find Black Beauty.
____ b. Black Beauty is sent away for acting badly.
____ c. Reuben is no longer working at the bar.
____ d. Reuben is dead and Black Beauty is badly hurt.

9. Another name for this story could be
____ a. "Beauty and the White Lion."
____ b. "Saying Good-bye is Hard."
____ c. "A New Way of Life."
____ d. "A Night to Remember."

10. This story is mainly about
____ a. getting used to a new place.
____ b. how different kinds of people act.
____ c. the owner of the White Lion.
____ d. saying good-bye to someone you love.

Check your answers with the key on page 67.

MY NEW HOME

VOCABULARY CHECK

band	crawl	listen	visit	whale	world

I. Sentences to Finish

Fill in the blank in each sentence with the correct key word from the box above.

1. We try to _____ to all kinds of music.

2. I am going to _____ my friend in the city.

3. The _____ on my watch keeps it tight on my arm.

4. The baby likes to _____ on the kitchen floor.

5. A _____ is a large animal that lives in the sea.

6. I would like to take a trip around the _____.

II. Making Sense of Sentences

Put a check next to <u>Yes</u> if the sentence makes sense. Put a check to <u>No</u> if the sentence does not make sense.

1. I like to <u>listen</u> to the birds sing in the morning. ___Yes ___No

2. The children had to <u>crawl</u> through the small hole in the wall. ___Yes ___No

3. Susan put a <u>band</u> in the pot and turned on the stove. ___Yes ___No

4. Mark will <u>visit</u> me after school today. ___Yes ___No

5. The <u>world</u> fell off the shelf. ___Yes ___No

6. A <u>whale</u> lives in a tree near my house. ___Yes ___No

Check your answers with the key on page 70.

MY LIFE AS A JOB HORSE

PREPARATION

Key Words

branch	(branch)	a part of a tree *The cat sat on a high <u>branch</u> in the old tree and waited for a bird.*
need	(nēd)	to be in want of; cannot do without *I <u>need</u> a new book for school.*
smell	(smel)	what your nose does *I love to <u>smell</u> the flowers in the garden.*
strong	(strông)	to be able to lift or carry heavy things *One must be <u>strong</u> to pick up a box full of rocks.*
supper	(sup ′ pər)	evening meal *It's nice to eat <u>supper</u> with your family.*
wonderful	(wun ′ dər fəl)	very good *I feel <u>wonderful</u> when I run in the park.*

MY LIFE AS A JOB HORSE

Animals

Peggy   is a pretty girl horse that pulls the wagon with Black Beauty.

Rory   is a horse that gets hurt while pulling the wagon with Black Beauty.

Things

steam engine   is a fast train run by steam.

MY LIFE AS A JOB HORSE

Ginger and I said good-bye and I was on my way to a new home.

Preview:
1. Read the name of the story.
2. Look at the picture.
3. Read the sentence under the picture.
4. Read the first paragraph of the story.
5. Then answer the following question.

You learned from your preview that
____ a. Black Beauty was turned out in the fields to rest and get better.
____ b. Black Beauty would never be able to run or pull a carriage again.
____ c. Black Beauty did not like being out in the field.
____ d. Black Beauty wanted to get away from this place.

Turn to the Comprehension Check on page 40 for the right answer.

Now read the story

Read to find out where Black Beauty will go and what he will find there.

MY LIFE AS A JOB HORSE

As time went by, my foot got better and my legs got strong enough to walk on. I was turned out into the fields on the farm. The soft grass felt good on my feet and there was a pleasing smell to the flowers. I would reach for apples from a branch of a big, old apple tree.

There was one thing that I missed. I had a need to talk to someone.

One morning, Ginger was let out to run with me. We were so happy to see one another! We ran around and had a wonderful time. After supper, Ginger and I had a long talk.

When it was hot, we would stand under a large branch to get the sun off our backs. One day, my master came to take me away. Ginger and I said good-bye.

I went by train to a new barn. The first night, I could smell my supper coming. I was glad the food was good here. The horses that lived here were called job horses. People would give the master money for the horses to do work for them. It was here that I found there are many kinds of drivers. I will tell you about some of them.

First there are the tight-rein drivers. They hold onto the reins as hard as they can. The horse has no free play with his head.

Then there are the loose-rein drivers. They just let the reins go lightly on our backs and do not help us make our way at all.

Another kind of driver is the steam-engine driver. He thinks that horses are like steam engines, and can go just as fast as engines do. When they first take us out, they whip us. When they want to stop, they pull hard on the reins. Sometimes, the pull is so strong we almost get knocked off our feet.

A horse named Rory would ride next to me when I was on one of my steam-engine rides. One time our driver had to pull fast to get out of the way of another horse. Rory went down. He never pulled the wagon with me again.

Soon, another horse came to ride with me. Her name was Peggy. Peggy was a very pretty horse, but I did not like riding with her. She had very short legs and could not keep up with a horse that had long legs like mine.

There were times when I had some good driving here. One day I was put into a light carriage and taken to a house on a nearby street. A man came out. After looking me over, he took off my check rein. I felt so free! It was wonderful to have a driver behind me who could drive a horse the right way. It was just like old times.

The man took a liking to me. He talked to my master and said he had a friend who needed a good horse for riding.

I was on my way to another new home.

MY LIFE AS A JOB HORSE

COMPREHENSION CHECK

Choose the best answer.

1. Black Beauty missed
   ____ a. picking apples from trees.
   ____ b. running in the fields.
   ____ c. having someone to talk to.
   ____ d. riding with Lady Anne.

2. Job horses
   ____ a. were horses that were saved for special jobs on the farm.
   ____ b. were only given out to good drivers.
   ____ c. were taken out by people who gave money for them to do jobs.
   ____ d. were given the best care by their masters.

3. Tight-rein drivers
   ____ a. hold the reins tightly, but let the horse run free.
   ____ b. hold the reins so tight that they pull on the horse's head.
   ____ c. help the horse find its way along the road.
   ____ d. make one horse do the work of ten horses.

4. The driver that does not help the horse make its way is
   ____ a. the steam-engine driver.
   ____ b. the tight-rein driver.
   ____ c. the wagon driver.
   ____ d. the loose-rein driver.

5. The steam-engine driver
   ____ a. whips the horse and pulls hard on the reins.
   ____ b. makes the horse pull trains.
   ____ c. always yells and kicks the horse.
   ____ d. knocks the horse over if it doesn't do what he says.

6. Most of the people who used job horses
   ____ a. loved the animals very much.
   ____ b. did not care about the animals.
   ____ c. bought them after they used them.
   ____ d. felt sorry for the animals.

7. Rory
   ____ a. was badly hurt from his fall.
   ____ b. was a steam-engine driver.
   ____ c. pulled the wagon with Peggy.
   ____ d. was not a fast horse.

8. Black Beauty was on his way to a new home because
   ____ a. he looked like a cab horse.
   ____ b. the master's friend needed a horse to work on his farm.
   ____ c. someone needed a horse to race.
   ____ d. a nice man had a friend who needed a good riding horse.

9. Another name for this story could be
   ____ a. "Getting Used to Wagons."
   ____ b. "Life as a Steam-Engine Driver."
   ____ c. "Hard Times."
   ____ d. "Growing Old."

10. This story is mainly about
   ____ a. dealing with hard work and rough people.
   ____ b. working on a farm.
   ____ c. breaking down when things get rough.
   ____ d. learning to like people.

Check your answers with the key on page 67.

MY LIFE AS A JOB HORSE

VOCABULARY CHECK

| branch | smell | strong | supper | wonderful | need |

I. Sentences to Finish

Fill in the blank in each sentence with the correct key word from the box above.

1. I can_____the hamburgers cooking.

2. The_____man in the circus can lift an elephant.

3. We are having meat and potatoes for_____.

4. There are a lot of berries on the_____of that tree.

5. That dress looks_____on you.

6. I_____a new pair of shoes for work.

II. Cross Word Puzzle

Use the words from the box above to fill in the puzzle. Use the meanings below to help you choose the right words.

Across

1. what your nose does

3. very good

5. a part of a tree

Down

1. able to lift heavy things

2. cannot do without

4. evening meal

Check your answers with the key on page 70.

This page may be reproduced for classroom use.

THE THIEF

PREPARATION

Key Words

arm	(ärm)	the part of the body between the shoulder and the hand *The woman held on to the man's <u>arm</u> while crossing the street.*
bad	(bad)	not good *There was a <u>bad</u> smell in the house after the fire.*
because	(bi kôz´)	to say why *I like my teacher <u>because</u> he is so kind.*
early	(ėr´ lē)	before time *Even though we got to the show <u>early</u>, we had to stand on a long line.* the beginning part *My father goes fishing in the <u>early</u> morning.*
food	(füd)	things to eat *I put all the <u>food</u> in a picnic basket before we left.*
shout	(shout)	to talk loud; to yell *Please <u>shout</u> a little louder because I can't hear you over all the noise.*

THE THIEF

Necessary Words

understand	(un dər stand ′)	get the meaning of; know
		I understand why you feel sad today.

Things

corn	is a grain that is yellow in color and is used to feed animals.
hay	is grass that has been dried out.
oat	is a grain that is used to feed animals.

THE THIEF

I was not getting the right food or care and I began to get sick.

Preview:
1. Read the name of the story.
2. Look at the picture.
3. Read the sentence under the picture.
4. Read the first two paragraphs of the story.
5. Then answer the following question.

You learned from your preview that Black Beauty's new master
____ a. was a doctor.
____ b. had a barn built just for him.
____ c. was a good and kind man.
____ d. knew about horses.

Turn to the Comprehension Check on page 46 for the right answer.

Now read the story.

Read to find out why Black Beauty was not being cared for in the right way.

THE THIEF

My new master lived alone. He made enough money to make him happy. His doctor told him that horseback riding would be good for him. I would fit his needs just right.

My master did not know much about horses, but he was kind to me. He saw to it that I went to a good barn. My master told the barn master to give me the best food he could get.

The first two or three days I had much to eat. I had oats and corn. The barn master cleaned the barn and rubbed me down early each day. After a time, I got more grass to eat than corn. I began to get sick and I was not as lively as before.

I would have loved to shout to my master and tell him he was being taken in. I could not understand why he did not see that something was not right with me.

Early one morning, we went to visit a friend of my master. His friend looked at me and said I seemed very sick. I was very wet, but we had not been riding fast. He told my master to look into the barn and see to it that I was getting enough to eat. He said many bad men will take the food right out of the horse's mouth.

If horses could only talk, I would have told my master where my food was going. Each morning, the barn master would bring his boy into the room where the corn box was. The boy would put my corn and oats into a bag. Then he would run off with the bag on his arm.

One day, a policeman came in and saw the boy. He shouted for him to stop. The policeman took the boy by the arm and led him to the corn box. There they saw what he had done. The boy and my barn master were taken into town.

I got a new barn master. He was a good-looking man and took more time on his looks than he did on me. He put me into a loose box, but never took the time to clean it out. He never took the hay away. Soon there was a bad smell from what was under the hay. The strong smell made me so sick that I could not eat my food.

One day, my master came in and said the barn smelled. He told the barn master to clean it out and water it down. The barn master did nothing.

My feet started to get bad again because I never got out of my box to run. My food was not right and I got sick. I had to take horse balls, which were hard to get down.

The horse doctor looked at me. He said I was in a bad way. All of this came from not cleaning my box each day.

Soon, I started to get the right food again and my box was clean. I was on the road to being a happy, lively horse again. But my master was unhappy because he had been taken in by two bad barn masters. He believed that he should not have a horse.

When my feet were better, I was on my way to another home.

THE THIEF

COMPREHENSION CHECK

> **Preview Answer:**
>
> c. was a good and kind man.

Choose the best answer.

1. The first few days in his new home, Black Beauty was fed
    _____ a. grass.
    _____ b. oats and corn.
    _____ c. only corn.
    _____ d. very little.

2. Black Beauty knew that the barn master
    _____ a. was not being fair to his owner.
    _____ b. wanted to take him home for his son.
    _____ c. did not really like him.
    _____ d. was trying to make him sick.

3. The barn master was
    _____ a. keeping the corn and oats for his animals.
    _____ b. giving Black Beauty's food to other horses.
    _____ c. selling Black Beauty's food in town.
    _____ d. not really a barn master; but a horse thief.

4. Black Beauty thought his second barn master
    _____ a. was an honest and good-looking man.
    _____ b. was not really suited for his job.
    _____ c. didn't care about the way he looked.
    _____ d. would be just right for the job.

5. The two barn masters
    _____ a. tried hard to do their jobs well.
    _____ b. wanted to buy the barn from the owner.
    _____ c. cared more about themselves than the horses.
    _____ d. told Black Beauty's owner the real story.

6. Black Beauty got sick because
    _____ a. his box was never clean and he did not get out to run.
    _____ b. the barn master put something in the food.
    _____ c. the horse balls he had to take were too big.
    _____ d. his master rode him too hard and fast.

7. Black Beauty's owner was unhappy
    _____ a. because he could not take his horse out for a ride.
    _____ b. when he could find no buyers for his horse.
    _____ c. when the doctor charged him a lot of money.
    _____ d. because he had been taken in by two bad men.

8. Black Beauty
    _____ a. never forgot what his mother told him.
    _____ b. was not able to feel sad.
    _____ c. did not listen to what his mother had said.
    _____ d. will never like people again.

9. Another name for this story could be
    _____ a. "What to Do for a Sick Horse."
    _____ b. "No Food for Black Beauty."
    _____ c. "One Good Man and Two Bad Ones."
    _____ d. "Caring for Horses the Right Way."

10. This story is mainly about
    _____ a. a man and his son, who are wanted by the police.
    _____ b. a man who enjoys his horse.
    _____ c. taking care of a barn.
    _____ d. how men can be bad to animals and each other.

Check your answers with the key on page 67.

THE THIEF

VOCABULARY CHECK

arm	bad	because	early	food	shout

I. Sentences to Finish

Fill in the blank in each sentence with the correct key word from the box above.

1. The ball game had to be stopped_____it started to rain.

2. Eric hurt his_____playing football.

3. The milk went_____because it wasn't kept cold.

4. It was so noisy that we had to_____to be heard.

5. We will go to the beach_____in the morning before it gets too crowded.

6. There was a lot of_____at the dinner party.

II. Matching

Write the letter of the correct meaning from Column B next to the key word in Column A.

Column A	Column B
_____ 1. arm	a. not good
_____ 2. shout	b. things to eat
_____ 3. bad	c. to yell
_____ 4. food	d. the beginning part
_____ 5. early	e. to say why
_____ 6. because	f. the part of the body between the shoulder and the hand

Check your answers with the key on page 71.

A HORSE FAIR

PREPARATION

Key Words

finish   (fin ′ ish)   to do something to the end
You must finish your homework tonight.

kitchen   (kich ′ ən)   a room where food is kept and meals are made
The kitchen has the smell of newly baked cookies.

later   (lāt ′ ər)   after a while; not right now
The television show I like to watch will be on later.

left   (left)   not taken
John left his books at school.
opposite of right
I use my left hand to write.

poor   (pur)   not having much money
The poor man stood on the street asking people to drop money in his hat.
unlucky
The poor child hurt his arm when he fell off his bike.

sign   (sīn)   something that tells us about a thing or person
The redness in her face was a sign of her sickness.
a board with writing on it
There is a sign on the corner of our street that tells the name of the block.

A HORSE FAIR

Necessary Words

cab (kab)   a carriage pulled by a horse with a driver, that people pay for to be taken somewhere
The cab picked the man up at his home.

war (wôr)   fighting between men or countries
Many men are hurt or killed in a war.

People

Jerry Barker   is the man who bought Black Beauty at the horse fair.

Places

horse fair   is where people go to look at and buy horses.

Animals

Captain   is a cab horse that lives in the barn with Black Beauty at Jerry Barker's place. Captain was ridden in the war by a man in charge of the fighting.

Jack   is the new name given to Black Beauty by the Barker family.

A HORSE FAIR

Jerry Barker's family gave me cookies and loving pats.

Preview:
1. Read the name of the story.
2. Look at the picture.
3. Read the sentence under the picture.
4. Read the first three paragraphs of the story.
5. Then answer the following question.

You learned from your preview that

_____ a. only old horses are shown at horse fairs.

_____ b. people do not touch horses at horse fairs.

_____ c. a horse's legs are not very important.

_____ d. horses do not like going to horse fairs.

Turn to the Comprehension Check on page 52 for the right answer.

Now read the story.

Read to find out what Black Beauty's job will be at the Barkers' place.

A HORSE FAIR

I was taken to a horse fair so that someone could buy me. This may be fun for people, but not for horses.

There are all kinds of horses at a horse fair. Some horses are big, while others are small. Some animals are old, and others are very good-looking.

I was put next to two big, strong horses. Many people came to look at us. The first thing they did was pull my mouth open. Then they would run their hands down my poor, old left leg and then my right one. Some of them would walk away when they felt my bad legs.

A man by the name of Jerry Barker took me home. He was a kind, happy man with a love for horses. Jerry was not poor, but he did not have much money to buy more than he needed.

When we got to his house, a fine-looking woman ran out of the kitchen. Behind her was a boy and a little girl. They all walked me to a small barn yard.

The children petted me. Then they left me just long enough to get apples and cookies from the kitchen. Later, they put me in a clean-smelling barn. Jerry's wife gave me a new name. I would be called Jack, after the horse that had come before me. At the finish of a good supper, I went to sleep thinking that I would be very happy in this place.

Jerry and I got along right away. He had a way with people as much as he did with horses. Jerry had a cab and another horse named Captain.

My first days as a cab horse were very trying. I had never been on streets like the ones in this town. There was a sign on each street, and one street was more full than the next.

I had as much food and love as any horse could want. The best thing about being here was that Jerry did not think anyone had to work on Sunday—man or horse. He believed it was good to have a day with his family.

On Sundays, Captain would tell me war stories. He would finish one and go right on to another. I liked to listen to him.

One Sunday, Jerry had to take out the cab. We took a lady to see her sick mother. Jerry followed one sign after another to get us out of the city. Soon, grass lands were all around us.

As we waited for the lady to visit with her mother, Jerry took the reins off me. He let me out in a big field. I did not know what to do first. I wanted to run all around, eat the grass and have fun. I was so happy to be free to run in the grass again!

Jerry was happy too. He sat under a big tree and listened to the birds sing. Then he read from his book. Later, when we got home, Jerry said he had not lost his Sunday after all. It had been a very good day.

A HORSE FAIR

COMPREHENSION CHECK

Choose the best answer.

1. At the horse fair there were
   _____ a. only race horses.
   _____ b. only small horses.
   _____ c. only young, fresh horses.
   _____ d. many kinds of horses.

2. Black Beauty's legs
   _____ a. were still as strong as when he was a young horse.
   _____ b. were what stopped him from being a good cab horse.
   _____ c. had been hurt because of men's thoughtless acts.
   _____ d. had been bad since the day he was born.

3. The first thing people did when they looked at Black Beauty was
   _____ a. check his legs.
   _____ b. open his mouth.
   _____ c. walk around him.
   _____ d. touch his neck.

4. Jerry Barker was a man who
   _____ a. would give Black Beauty a good home.
   _____ b. treated horses and people badly.
   _____ c. had a lot of money.
   _____ d. was very poor.

5. Jerry's wife named Black Beauty
   _____ a. Captain.
   _____ b. Jack.
   _____ c. Mother.
   _____ d. Sunday.

6. Black Beauty
   _____ a. could not get along with Captain.
   _____ b. only listened to Jerry Barker.
   _____ c. did not think he would like his new home at first.
   _____ d. worked very hard for Jerry, but did not mind.

7. For Black Beauty, the best thing about living on Jerry's farm was
   _____ a. eating all the apples and cookies he wanted.
   _____ b. Jerry's thinking that girl horses should not work hard.
   _____ c. pulling the cab through busy streets.
   _____ d. not having to work on Sundays.

8. When Jerry had to work one Sunday, he
   _____ a. was sad and did not talk the whole day.
   _____ b. would not take the reins off Jack.
   _____ c. made the best of the day in the country.
   _____ d. told the lady she had to pay more.

9. Another name for this story could be
   _____ a. "Jack and Jerry in Town."
   _____ b. "A Happy New Home."
   _____ c. "A New Name for Beauty."
   _____ d. "A Day at the Fair."

10. This story is mainly about
    _____ a. Black Beauty's life with a kind man.
    _____ b. different kinds of horses.
    _____ c. the many people who go to horse fairs.
    _____ d. Black Beauty's thoughts about the city.

Check your answers with the key on page 67.

A HORSE FAIR

VOCABULARY CHECK

| finish | kitchen | later | left | poor | sign |

I. Sentences to Finish

Fill in the blank in each sentence with the correct key word from the box above.

1. When we_____dinner, we will have dessert.

2. Margie is in the_____baking a cake.

3. We will go to Susan's house_____.

4. Paul_____before we could finish the game.

5. The family is so_____that they cannot buy coats for the winter.

6. The_____on the door of the store said it was closed.

II. Making Sense of Sentences

Put a check next to YES if the sentence makes sense. Put a check next to NO if the sentence does not make sense.

1. Paula <u>left</u> the house in a hurry.

   _____ Yes   _____ No

2. If you <u>finish</u> something, you have just started.

   _____ Yes   _____ No

3. The family was <u>poor</u> because they had a lot of money and goods.

   _____ Yes   _____ No

4. Grandmother is cooking in the <u>kitchen</u>.

   _____ Yes   _____ No

5. A cloudy day is a <u>sign</u> of bad weather.

   _____ Yes   _____ No

6. I will be going to Bob's house <u>later</u>.

   _____ Yes   _____ No

Check your answers with the key on page 71.

MY LIFE AS A CAB HORSE

PREPARATION

Key Words

dirty	(dėr ′ tē)	not clean
		Please wash your <u>dirty</u> hands before you sit down to eat.
feather	(feᴛʜ ′ ər)	part of the wing of a bird
		The bird has one red <u>feather</u> on its wing.
felt	(felt)	to have had a feeling
		I <u>felt</u> sad when I heard you were sick.
great	(grāt)	very important; very good
		We had a <u>great</u> time at the picnic.
maybe	(mā ′ bē)	it may be
		<u>Maybe</u> we will go to the show when we finish our work.
sheep	(shēp)	an animal raised for wool and food
		The <u>sheep</u> is a quiet animal.

MY LIFE AS A CAB HORSE

Necessary Words

crash (krash) a falling, hitting or breaking with force and a loud noise
The plane crash took the lives of many people.

hospital (hos ′ pi təl) a place where sick people are taken care of
I am going to the hospital to visit my sick aunt.

station (stā ′ shən) a place where people stand to wait for a cab or train
The cab station was full of people and horses all waiting to go to a special place.

vote (vōt) the choosing of a person who will act for the people in the government of the land
The person who gets my vote will believe in the same things that I do.

People

Seedy Sam is a poor cab driver.

MY LIFE AS A CAB HORSE

I could not believe what I was seeing. The old, tired-looking horse next to me was my old friend.

Preview:
1. Read the name of the story.
2. Look at the picture.
3. Read the sentences under the picture.
4. Read the first paragraph of the story.
5. Then answer the following question.

You learned from your preview that
____ a. all cab drivers like their work.
____ b. not all cab horses were taken care of as well as Black Beauty.
____ c. the cab station was a happy, fun place to work.
____ d. cab driving was a great way to make a living.

Turn to the Comprehension Check on page 58 for the right answer.

Now read the story.

Read to find out who Black Beauty's old friend is and what has happened since their last meeting.

MY LIFE AS A CAB HORSE

It was great living with Jerry Barker as his cab horse. Not all horses were taken care of like I was. I was never overworked and I was clean all the time. I felt just great. But when I looked around the cab station, I was sad. There were dirty men and overworked horses everywhere. Some of the drivers had a hard time making a living. They were as overworked as their horses.

One day, a dirty-looking man named Seedy Sam was saying bad things about cab driving. He said that for all his work, he was still a poor man. He could never get ahead. He had hardly any money to feed his family. After hearing his long talk, we all felt bad for him.

Some days later, I heard that Seedy Sam got very sick and was now dead. He had worked too hard and it had taken the best out of him.

One day I was waiting near a park listening to my feathered friends sing, when an overworked cab horse pulled up alongside me. The horse looked old and tired. I looked at it with sheep eyes. You could have knocked me over with a feather when I saw it was my old friend Ginger.

This was not the Ginger I had left behind. She told me her long, unhappy story about all the masters she had since the day we said good-bye in the field. Ginger said she wished she were dead. She could not go on living this way anymore. She told me I was the only friend she ever had.

Just then, her driver came up and pulled hard at her mouth. I watched her ride off and I felt sorry for her. A short time later, I saw a wagon go by with a dead horse in it. It looked like Ginger and I hoped it was. That would have been the best thing that could have happened to her.

The town was getting ready for the big vote. When the big day came, Jerry and I had more work than we could take on. We were driving all day. Jerry stopped to give me oats and water from time to time. This made the day better.

A woman came up to the stand and asked Jerry the way to the hospital. She was carrying a small, heavy child. The woman was poor and she was going to walk all the way. But Jerry took her there without taking any money.

One day the old Captain was gone. There had been a cab crash. I was like a little lost sheep without the Captain to talk to. Jerry got another horse right away. We made friends very fast.

Maybe Christmas and the New Year is a happy time for most people. For a cab driver and his horse, it is a time for hard work. We worked so many cold nights that Jerry soon got very sick. When he got better, the doctor told him to give up his cab work.

Jerry and his family went to a new home where he would be a barn driver. I was off again to a new place.

MY LIFE AS A CAB HORSE

COMPREHENSION CHECK

Preview Answer:

b. not all cab horses were taken
   care of as well as Black Beauty.

Choose the best answer.

1. Black Beauty felt bad for Seedy Sam because
    _____ a. he was overworked and poor.
    _____ b. he had no family.
    _____ c. no one liked him.
    _____ d. he was sick and couldn't hear.

2. The horse that pulled up beside "Jack" near the park was
    _____ a. Merrylegs.
    _____ b. Captain.
    _____ c. Rory.
    _____ d. Ginger.

3. Black Beauty thought Ginger
    _____ a. was making life hard for herself.
    _____ b. was only saying she was not happy.
    _____ c. would be better off dead.
    _____ d. looked quite good at her age.

4. For most, life as a cab horse was
    _____ a. easy.
    _____ b. a hard life.
    _____ c. fun.
    _____ d. a good life.

5. On the voting day, Jerry stopped from time to time
    _____ a. to give Black Beauty oats and water.
    _____ b. because he could not take all the work.
    _____ c. so he could talk to his friends.
    _____ d. to call his family at home.

6. Jerry showed his kindness when
    _____ a. he took a woman and child to the hospital, but would take no money.
    _____ b. he charged a man half of what he usually would have charged.
    _____ c. he let a young boy ride on Black Beauty.
    _____ d. he would not take too many bags in the cab.

7. Jerry got sick because
    _____ a. he had to work many cold nights during the holiday.
    _____ b. he stayed out too long at the horse fair.
    _____ c. he was tired and poor.
    _____ d. he was stuck in a storm.

8. Black Beauty
    _____ a. would always stay with Jerry.
    _____ b. would be going to a new home.
    _____ c. would stay at Jerry's home with the new owner.
    _____ d. would be happy to leave Jerry and cab work.

9. Another name for this story could be
    _____ a. "Back on the Farm Again."
    _____ b. "Working with Ginger."
    _____ c. "Jerry Barker's Story."
    _____ d. "Hard Work on City Streets."

10. This story is mainly about
    _____ a. getting used to working on the farm.
    _____ b. a sad life for Black Beauty.
    _____ c. the different kinds of people you meet in the city.
    _____ d. Black Beauty's experience as a cab horse in the city.

Check your answers with the key on page 67.

MY LIFE AS A CAB HORSE

VOCABULARY CHECK

dirty	feather	felt	great	maybe	sheep

I. Sentences to Finish

Fill in the blank in each sentence with the correct key word from the box above.

1. The car was very_____after being driven through the muddy street.

2. The farmer will shave each of the_____for its woolly coat.

3. _____we can go to the library after school.

4. A_____pillow is very soft.

5. I think your new game is_____fun!

6. I_____happy when my friends came to see me in the hospital.

II. Word Search

All the words from the box above are hidden in the puzzle below. They may be written from left to right or up and down. As you find each word, put a circle around it. One word, that is not a key word, has been done for you.

```
W F D X Y F A C V
O P S D T E Q R U
M N F R E L T S K
W A F E A T H E R
A B G A D C H I J
S A I D R P O R T
H E R I O G R A P
E M L R A S C I H
E T U T G R E A T
P M A Y B E P A E
```

Check your answers with the key on page 71.

MY LAST HOME

PREPARATION

Key Words

hope	(hōp)	a strong wish for something *I hope to make some friends in my new neighborhood.*
jolly	(jol ′ ē)	full of fun; happy *Santa Claus is a jolly man with a bright smile.*
lion	(lī ′ ən)	a big wild animal belonging to the cat family *At the circus we saw a man put his head in the mouth of a lion.*
sky	(skī)	the air above the earth *There are some beautiful white clouds in the sky today.*
song	(sông)	words and music together *When I feel happy, I sing a song.*
stairs	(sterz)	a set of steps going from one floor to another *One should always hold on to the railing when going up or down the stairs.*

MY LAST HOME

Necessary Words

load   (lōd)   things placed on a person, animal, wagon, truck, etc. to be carried

The wagon brought a <u>load</u> of hay to the barn.

strength   (strengkth, strength)   to be strong

You will need all your <u>strength</u> to lift that heavy box.

MY LAST HOME

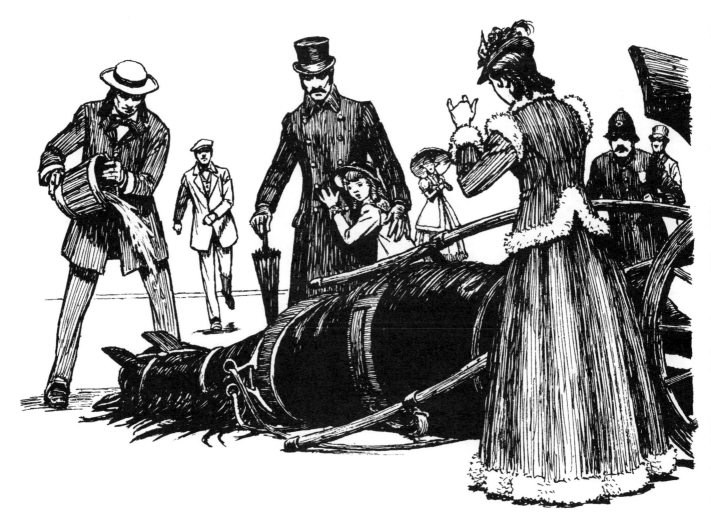

I was going along fine when my legs gave way. Suddenly, I was down on the ground.

Preview:
1. Read the name of the story.
2. Look at the picture.
3. Read the sentences under the picture.
4. Read the first two paragraphs of the story.
5. Then answer the following question.

You learned from your preview that Black Beauty
_____ a. would have another nice home.
_____ b. would do the work he was meant to do.
_____ c. faced another difficult time in his life.
_____ d. was about to find a good and kind man.

Turn to the Comprehension Check on page 64 for the right answer.

Now read the story.

Read to find out if Black Beauty will ever see happy days again.

MY LAST HOME

A corn farmer came and bought me for very little money. All his horses were overworked. We had too much to carry for too long a time.

One day I was pulling a big load up a high hill. If only there had been stairs for my driver to walk up so he could have lightened my load. He used a whip on me. I felt very bad because I was doing the best I could.

Just as I was about to be whipped again, a kind lady walked up. She told the driver to take off my checkrein. He did so. It felt great to look down at the ground and up at the sky. I got my strength back and pulled the load up the hill.

Soon my legs got so bad that a younger horse had to come and take my job. A short time later, a cab master came to buy me. I did not like him. He had black eyes and a mouth like a lion.

My job as a cab horse had been good before. With my new master, the job was hard and the days were too long. I was whipped all the time. There was never a song in my heart. I would look up at the sky and hope that soon I would join Ginger in a resting place.

My wish very nearly came true one day. I was at the cab station. I had done a full day's work when a train pulled in. A family of four came near our cab. The little girl told her father that the family and all their bags would be more than I could pull. My driver said this was not so.

I had not had food or water for a long time. I was going along and trying hard when my legs gave way. I heard someone say that I was dead and would never get up again. I don't know how long I was down. Someone threw cold water on my head. Then a kind man got me up on my feet and walked me to a barn.

The horse doctor told my master that with food, and time off from work, I would be good enough to sell. Some days later, a little boy and his grandfather came and took me home. I had good food at their place. My legs got better and I felt strong as a lion again. I was jolly once more.

One day I was taken to a pretty house where three ladies lived. A young barn master walked me to the barn. He saw the white star on my head and my one white foot.

"It's Black Beauty!" he cried out. "Why, Beauty, do you know me? I'm little Joe Green that almost killed you."

I could not say that I remembered him. Now he was a strong young man. I put my nose up to him and tried to say we were friends. I never saw a man so pleased.

I have been here for a long time now. My ladies say I will never have to go away. This is my home, and I am as jolly as any horse could hope to be.

MY LAST HOME

COMPREHENSION CHECK

Preview Answer:

c. faced another difficult time in his life.

Choose the best answer.

1. First, Black Beauty was bought by
   _____ a. a rich lady.
   _____ b. a corn farmer.
   _____ c. a gentle driver.
   _____ d. a little girl.

2. Having a younger horse take his place
   _____ a. made Black Beauty very happy.
   _____ b. must have made Black Beauty feel sad and angry.
   _____ c. did not make any difference to Black Beauty.
   _____ d. left Black Beauty to do easier work.

3. Black Beauty did not like his new cab master because
   _____ a. he was a mean man.
   _____ b. he did not like people.
   _____ c. he would always sing in a loud voice.
   _____ d. he wanted to send Black Beauty away.

4. While working as a cab horse this time, Black Beauty
   _____ a. lost his will to live.
   _____ b. was still able to see happy days ahead.
   _____ c. was sorry that Ginger was not still working.
   _____ d. found life much easier.

5. Soon after leaving the cab station,
   _____ a. the cab driver became sick and had to stop.
   _____ b. all the bags fell off the cab.
   _____ c. Black Beauty lost a shoe and tripped.
   _____ d. Black Beauty fell to the ground.

6. A little boy and his grandfather
   _____ a. sold Black Beauty to a cab driver.
   _____ b. took good care of Black Beauty.
   _____ c. knew that Joe Green had cared for Black Beauty.
   _____ d. gave Black Beauty to an old barn master.

7. The barn master at Black Beauty's new home was
   _____ a. Squire Gordon.
   _____ b. John.
   _____ c. Joe Green.
   _____ d. Jerry Barker.

8. Black Beauty's life
   _____ a. was full of happiness.
   _____ b. ended in sadness.
   _____ c. began in a bad way.
   _____ d. was a hard one.

9. Another name for this story could be
   _____ a. "Back at Squire Gordon's."
   _____ b. "A Sad Ending."
   _____ c. "Joe and Beauty—Together Again."
   _____ d. "Life As a Fair Horse."

10. This story is mainly about
    _____ a. people in a small town.
    _____ b. life with Joe Green.
    _____ c. how hard work pays off on a corn farm.
    _____ d. how Black Beauty comes to meet a friend.

Check your answers with the key on page 67.

MY LAST HOME

VOCABULARY CHECK

hope	jolly	lion	sky	song	stairs

I. Sentences to Finish

Fill in the blank in each sentence with the correct key word from the box above.

1. I_____I get a new baseball bat for my birthday.

2. I like to listen to the words to a_____as well as the music.

3. The_____has a loud roar.

4. My bedroom is at the top of the_____.

5. The_____is full of stars tonight.

6. A clown must be_____if he wants to make people laugh.

II. Finish the Story

Use the key words from the box above to finish the story below so that it makes sense.

Black Beauty would always_____that his next home would be a nice one. But it

was hard for him to keep a_____in his heart. Most of his owners were as mean as

a_____. At the end of the story Black Beauty has no more_____

to climb. He can look up at the_____and feel free at last. Joe Green will help

Black Beauty be_____once more.

Check your answers with the key on page 72.

NOTES